Classic Ships of the Great Lakes
by Robert B. Campbell

Copyright © 2015 by Robert Campbell

Published by
Thunder Bay Press
West Branch, MI 48661

ISBN: 978-1-933272-50-4
Library of Congress Control Number: 2015934846

First Edition 2015
Second Printing 2019

24 23 22 21   3 4 5 6

All photographs by the author except where credited.
Chapter illustrations by Robert McGreevy, author and artist of *Lost
    Legends of the Lakes*, ISBN 978-1-933272-48-1.
Book and cover design by Julie Taylor.

Printed in the United States of America

This book is dedicated to
Dorothy Wallin, the original
Port Huron "River Rat."

ABOVE: Sunset on Lake Superior from the *Kinsman Independent*

ACKNOWLEDGEMENTS

This book is a culmination of my lifelong interest in Great Lakes ships, which began with annual family trips to visit relatives at Sault Ste. Marie. I want to remember those who helped me along the way: My uncle Jerry Campbell, who worked forty years at the Soo Locks and always told stories about the boats. Tom Manse, the editor of the book *Know Your Ships*, who steered me from being a boat watcher to a boat photographer. Also, Roger Lelievre, who enhanced my photographic horizon and took me out in his motorboat for memorable moments on the St. Marys River. Ruth Stevens, a good friend, who worked at the Soo Locks administration building. I always enjoyed seeing her pictures of shipping at the Soo Locks and am proud to include a few of them in this book. Also, Dorothy Wallin, to whom I dedicate this book.

I am grateful to those who helped me with information. Those include Dick Wicklund, Dave Michelson, and Bob McGreevy. Thanks also to Jim Acheson and Mike Delong of Acheson Ventures of Port Huron, Michigan, who granted me access to the VanderLinden collection for maritime research. I want to acknowledge those who assisted me with pictures including Captain Paul Allers and Don Geske. Thanks also to Charles Graham and Steve Elve for their help.

Lastly, I want to thank Bill Harrison of Custom Photographic in Lansing, Michigan, as well as the publishers at Thunder Bay Press, in particular Julie Taylor for her work with the layout.

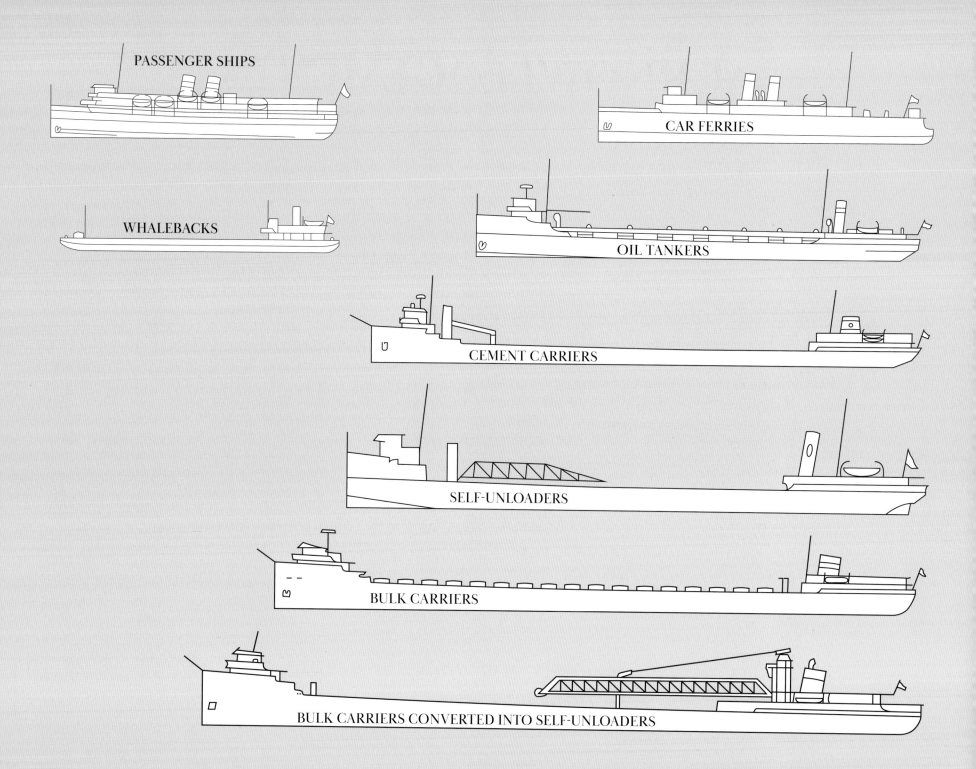

PASSENGER SHIPS

CAR FERRIES

WHALEBACKS

OIL TANKERS

CEMENT CARRIERS

SELF-UNLOADERS

BULK CARRIERS

BULK CARRIERS CONVERTED INTO SELF-UNLOADERS

TABLE OF CONTENTS

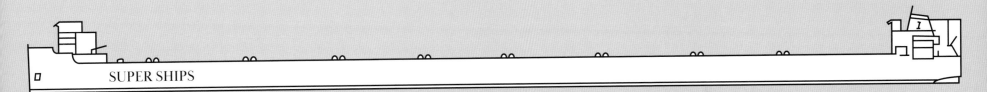

SUPER SHIPS

FOREWORD

If one were to look at the entire North American continent above the earth, the most recognizable feature would be the Great Lakes, including the St. Lawrence River connecting them with the north Atlantic Ocean. What a magnificent region is the Great Lakes, providing abundant resources for mankind!

From the beginning of transportation on the Great Lakes, vessels of all types were used to transport people, the most important cargo. Certainly the canoe and the sailing ship were predecessors and contemporaries in such trade with steamboats. As the conflict between the two nations bordering the Great Lakes, Canada and the United States, ended after the War of 1812, settlers and immigrants began to move into the region in greater numbers.

The first steamboats on the Great Lakes were the Canadian *Frontenac*, built in 1816, and the 1818 American-built *Walk-In-The-Water*. Other steamboats soon followed, since railroads were in their infancy and years from reaching the Great Lakes region. These early steamboats were wood-hulled, side-wheel ships with the engine in the middle of the hull, called walking beam engines, which were very tall and often exposed to the elements. Also, these steamships were used to accommodate both passengers and freight.

As America's population grew along the east coast, immigrants new to the continent and young settlers looking for more land moved westward. However, the Appalachian Mountains presented a major obstacle for them. In the northern part of this mountain range, between the Catskill and Adirondack Mountains in New York State, a canal was built in 1825, the Erie Canal. It connected Albany on the Hudson River with Buffalo on Lake Erie, enabling people to move from New York City, up the Hudson River and the Erie Canal, to the Great Lakes by water. There they could take a steamboat to either settle along its shores or use them to travel farther west by water.

It should be emphasized that between about 1830 and 1860, the Great Lakes region experienced phenomenal growth in population. Towns of five hundred to a thousand grew to cities of tens of thousands from Toronto, Buffalo, Cleveland, and Detroit west to Milwaukee, Chicago, and Duluth. Mobilization of people, along with their goods and products, meant the quick development of the steamboat.

Another type of steamboat was introduced, called a propeller, with a smaller engine in the stern, not in the middle, allowing for more passenger and cargo capacity. This screw propeller engine developed by John Ericsson was first used on the *Vandalia* on the Great Lakes in 1841. Both the side-wheel and the propeller steamboats would be used on the Great Lakes, with the propeller finding additional use in carrying larger bulk cargos. These were the predecessors of our modern bulk freighters on the Lakes.

The development of the propeller was just in time for the discovery and mining of the vast iron ore deposits in the northern Great Lakes region in the late 1840s. This directly resulted in the building of the locks at Sault Ste. Marie in 1855. Iron ore, however, was not the only bulk commodity to benefit from propeller steamers. Production of grain, lumber, coal, and various types of stone prospered as well.

During the last decades of the 1800s, the Great Lakes were the perfect route to fuel the Industrial Revolution and usher in the prosperous Victorian Age. The rich deposits of iron ore and limestone along the shores combined with coal from the Ohio River Valley created the steel mills along southern Lake Erie and Lake Michigan. This industry alone built cities in the U.S. and Canada, armaments for two World Wars, and the giant automobile industry. Great Lakes ships contributed to this growth—and more.

To cover the history of shipping so briefly is completely inadequate considering there are more than 400 years of Great Lakes shipping history! These are not just ships passing on the Great Lakes, each has a history and a heritage to remember.

It is with this purpose that *Classic Ships of the Great Lakes* is presented, to remind each generation that the Great Lakes, its people, and its 'long ships passing' have a story to tell.

—Dick Wicklund

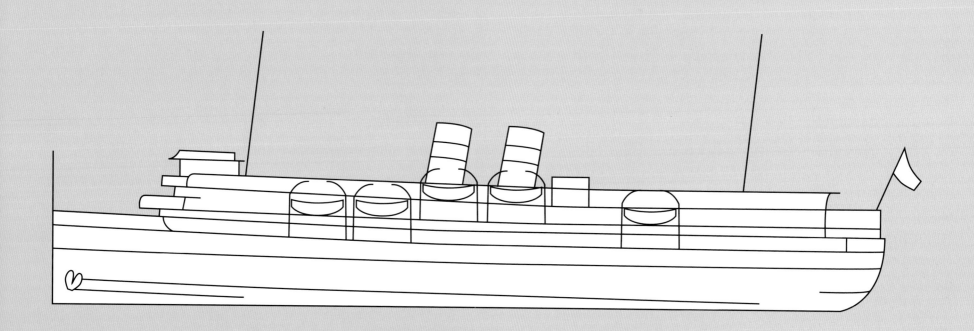

PASSENGER SHIPS

The history of passenger ship travel on the Great Lakes begins with the opening of the Erie Canal in 1825 from Albany to Buffalo which increased immigration to the region. The early steamers were small, of wooden construction, and rather fragile when faced with a lake tempest. In time, larger and stronger passenger ships were built. Notable steamers such as the *Detroit* and *Keystone State* had tall stacks and sidewheel propulsion.

In 1871 the first iron-hulled passenger ships were built, the triplets *India*, *China*, and *Japan*. They were some of the most beautiful vessels to sail the lakes. The Pennsylvania Railroad operated these vessels for the Anchor Line Company. These were later replaced by the *Tionesta* of 1903, *Juniata* of 1905, and *Octorara* of 1910. Besides carrying passengers, they engaged in the general freight business such as hauling copper from the Keweenaw Peninsula. Two of the finest passenger ships preceding the *Tionesta* were the *North West* of 1894 and *Northland* of 1895. They were built for James J. Hill, the famous "Empire Builder" for the Northern Navigation Company. Due to their sleek looks and elegant appointments, they were deemed twenty years ahead of their time.

The peak years for passenger boats was between 1900 and 1930 due in part to a huge increase in tourism. People wanted to escape the heavy industrial areas for the peace and tranquility of the northern Great Lakes. Shorter day excursions were also available. The *Tashmoo* out of Detroit took passengers to Tashmoo Park. The *Put-In-Bay* carried travelers to the Lake Erie Islands. The 1902-built *Columbia* and 1910 *Ste. Claire* would go to Bob-Lo Island amusement park. Both of these boats remained active through the 1991 season.

On the Canadian side, the *Keewatin* and *Assiniboia* of 1907 were the last two vessels Canadian Pacific built. The *Keewatin* ran until 1965 and presently resides as a museum in her old home, Port McNicoll, Ontario. The *Assiniboia* carried on through the 1967 season.

The Georgian Bay Line steamers *North* and *South American* of 1913 and 1914, respectively, gained in popularity during the heavy tourism years. The *North* sailed until 1964 while the *South* went through 1967, one of her busiest seasons taking passengers to Montreal for Expo67. Safety regulations after that season spelled her doom as her interior was of wooden construction.

Today, the classic liners are all gone with the exception of the museum ship *Keewatin*. She still sports the ornate wood interior and beautiful lines of the classic passenger vessels. The beautiful looks and deep-throated whistles are all but memories.

ABOVE: The *North West* of the Northern Steamship Company at the Soo in the 1890s.   PHOTO: *STEVE ELVE COLLECTION*

ABOVE: The *Keewatin*, circa 1910.   PHOTO: AUTHOR'S COLLECTION

ABOVE: The steamer *Ste. Claire* "Bob-Lo Boat," August 1991.

LEFT: The steamer *Columbia* "Bob-Lo Boat," August 1991.

ABOVE: *North American* and *South American* at Mackinac Island.   PHOTO: PAUL ALLERS

LEFT: *South American* leaving Holland.   PHOTO: DON GESKE SR.

FOLLOWING PAGE: *Assiniboia* at Soo Canada.   PHOTO: DON GESKE SR.

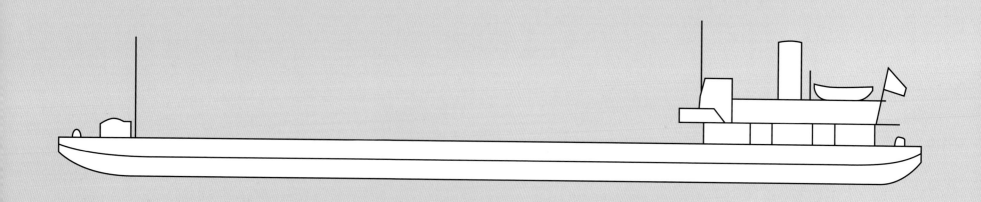

WHALEBACKS

The whalebacks were designed by Alexander McDougall, a Great Lakes captain, in the late 1800s. They were used to haul iron ore, coal, stone, and grain. Their looks represented a dramatic change from the conventional boat of the time. They had rounded, cigar-like hulls which tapered to a blunt-end resembling a pig snout. For this reason they were also known as "Pig Boats." During this time it was common practice for a steamer to tow one or two barges. Barges, especially the wood-hulled former schooners, were awkward to tow. McDougall felt the rounded hull design of his whalebacks, with flat bottoms, would cut through the water more smoothly.

The first of this type of vessel, *Barge 101*, was built in 1888 measuring 187 feet long. The decks were clear with the exception of two turrets on either end, housing towing and steering gear. While many sailors scoffed at the radical design of the new barge, it caught the eye of the Rockefeller shipping interests in Cleveland. They liked the design for hauling ore from the iron ranges of Minnesota to the lower lakes. The Rockefellers financed the building of many more whalebacks, both barges and steamers. This kept the shipyards in Superior, Wisconsin, across the harbor from Duluth, Minnesota, busy. In all, forty-two whalebacks were built between 1888 and 1898.

Most whalebacks had successful careers on the Great Lakes, but a few came to untimely ends. The steamer *Thomas Wilson* and *Barge 129* were lost by collision in 1902, each in Lake Superior. The steamer *James B. Colgate* foundered in the Black Friday storm in 1916 in Lake Erie, and the whaleback steamer the *Clifton*, formerly the *Samuel Mather*, foundered eight years later, in 1924, in Lake Huron. By the late 1940s, however, two whaleback steamers and a few barges were left. The *Meteor*, which came out as the steamer *Frank Rockefeller* in 1896 and was converted to an oil tanker in 1943, would be the last whaleback to survive. The *Meteor* was retired in 1970, and since 1972 it has functioned as a museum ship in Superior, Wisconsin, not far from where she was built.

ABOVE: The *Meteor*, formerly the *Frank Rockefeller* was the only whaleback converted to an oil tanker. She is shown at Grand Haven, Michigan, February 18, 1968.   PHOTO: DON GESKE SR.

LEFT: The *Frank Rockefeller*.   PHOTO: ACHESON VENTURES, VANDERLINDEN COLLECTION.

ABOVE: The *John Ericsson*.   PHOTO: ACHESON VENTURES, VANDERLINDEN COLLECTION.

RIGHT: The *John Ericsson* being lowered in the Soo Locks.   PHOTO: RUTH STEVENS

ABOVE: The *John Ericsson*, December 9, 1955.   PHOTO: RUTH STEVENS.

LEFT, TOP: The *John Ericsson*, summer 1960.   PHOTO: RUTH STEVENS.

LEFT, BOTTOM: The *John Ericsson* departing the locks, downbound.   PHOTO: RUTH STEVENS.

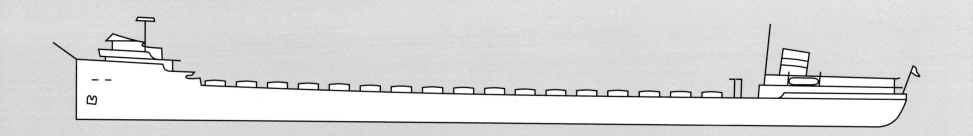

BULK CARRIERS

The first bulk freight carriers on the Great Lakes were the schooners. The principle cargoes were iron ore and coal to support the growing steel industry. Other cargoes were lumber and grain. The water system was the best means of transporting goods in those days.

The first Soo locks were opened in 1855 because vast amounts of iron ore deposits were discovered in the Lake Superior region. There was a need for carriers with more capacity. In 1869 Eli Peck designed a revolutionary vessel with pilot house forward and engines aft, the cargo hold comprising the center. The decks would be clear of the masts and rigging that a schooner needed and would make loading and unloading easier. The *R.J. Hackett*, a 200-foot wooden steamer, originated a design that became a mainstay of bulk carriers gracing our inland seas for years to come.

In time, newer and larger ships emerged to meet growing industry and population needs. The *Onoko* of 1882 would become the first boat constructed of iron and the *Spokane* of 1886 the first made of steel. By the end of the nineteenth century, vessel lengths were limited to 400 feet due to hull construction with support stanchions in the middle. The building of the *Augustus B. Wolvin* of 1904 featured a new arch type hull construction which added strength to the ship. This paved the way for longer ships. The support stanchions, which slowed the unloading process, were no longer needed. In 1906, the first 600 footers were built, and many of these sailed well into the 1970s. A few milestone freighters were the 1927-built *Harry Coulby* of Interlake Steamship at 631 feet long and the *Lemoyne* of 1926. At 633 feet long, 70 foot beam, and 33 foot depth, the *Lemoyne* was the largest ship of the Canadian fleet.

By 1949, the *Wilfred Sykes* at 678 feet long represented the ultimate of Great Lakes bulkers, a real Queen of the Lakes. Vessels continued to grow with the *Edmund Fitzgerald* of 1958 at 729 feet followed two years later by the *Edward L. Ryerson* at 730 feet.

The 1980s saw a downturn of the straight deck bulkers. Iron ore, once the staple cargo of the bulkers, would be converted to taconite pellets and better hauled by the self-unloading vessels. A few straight deck bulkers are still used in the grain business displaying their majestic profile as they plod along, but their numbers are growing fewer.

ABOVE: An early bulk freighter, the steamer *James A. Farrell* at the Soo.   PHOTO: ACHESON VENTURES, VANDERLINDEN COLLECTION.

RIGHT, TOP: The *William P. Snyder Jr.* in Cleveland-Cliffs colors.

RIGHT, BOTTOM: The *William P. Snyder Jr.* of the Shenango Fleet downbound at the Soo, June 1968.

ABOVE: The *Mantadoc* downbound at Port Huron, Michigan, with a load of grain for the lower St. Lawrence River port.

LEFT, TOP: The *Charles M. White* in Republic colors, 1968.

LEFT, BOTTOM: The *Charles M. White* of the Cleveland Cliffs fleet.

ABOVE AND LEFT: The steamer *Oakglen (1)*, formerly the *International*, sailing into a fog bank in the lower St. Marys River, 1983.

FAR LEFT: The *International* of the International Harvester fleet on the St. Marys River in July 1976.

ABOVE: The *Oakglen (2)*, formerly the *T.R. McLagan*, at the Welland Ship Canal in 1996.

RIGHT: The *Oakglen (1)*, formerly the *International*, at the rock cut in 1983. Sold for overseas scrapping 1988.

ABOVE: The *Henry Steinbrenner (3)* of the Kinsman fleet heading for Lake Huron in 1977.

RIGHT, TOP: The *Henry Steinbrenner (4)*, formerly the *William A. McGonagle*, at a Buffalo grain elevator 1987.

RIGHT, BOTTOM: The *Henry Steinbrenner (4)* in the rock cut.

ABOVE: The *Kinsman Enterprise (1)*, formerly *Norman B. Ream*, downbound under the Blue Water Bridge at Port Huron, Michigan.

ABOVE: The *Kinsman Independent (2)* all painted up below the Soo.

ABOVE: The *Edmund Fitzgerald* at the Soo, September 1969.

LEFT AND FAR LEFT: The *Edmund Fitzgerald*, May 1975.

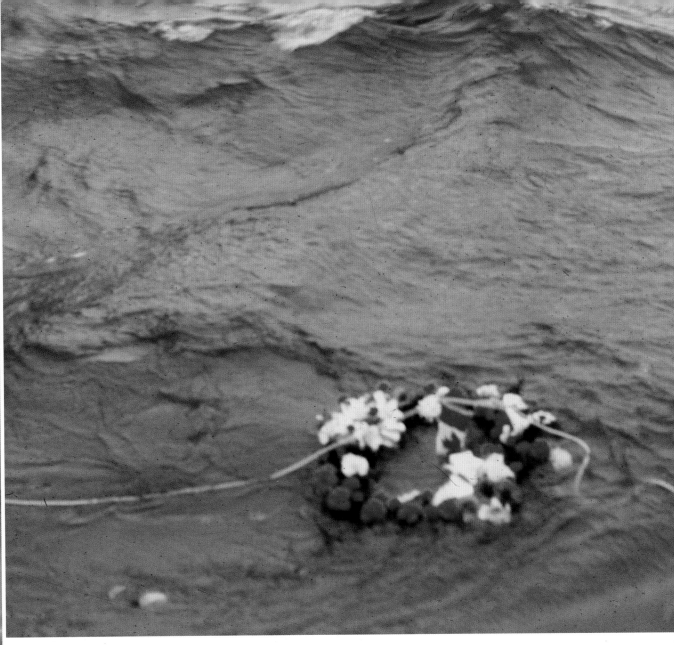

ABOVE: Wreath in the water.

LEFT: Canadian cutter *Verendrye* during the Wreath Ceremony for the *Edmund Fitzgerald*, Thanksgiving weekend 1975.

TOP LEFT: The *William P. Palmer* downbound at the Soo in 1969.

TOP RIGHT: The *Paul L. Teitjen* of the Kinsman Fleet.

BOTTOM LEFT: The *A. H. Ferbert* in the ice above the Soo Locks in 1980.

BOTTOM RIGHT: The *Peter A. B. Widener*, an early 600 footer in 1974.

ABOVE: The *Arthur B. Homer*, sister ship to the *Edmund Fitzgerald*, at the Soo in 1979.

ABOVE: The *George R. Fink* downbound at Mission Point, Sault Ste. Marie in September 1969.

LEFT: The *John Sherwin* on the St. Mary's River in May, 1977.

ABOVE: The *Benjamin F. Fairless* at the Soo, December 1976.

LEFT: The *Benjamin F. Fairless.*

TOP, LEFT AND RIGHT: The *Arthur M. Anderson* heads for Lake Superior in February 1978.

BOTTOM, LEFT AND RIGHT: The *Phillip D. Block*, 1979.

LEFT: The *Arthur M. Anderson* on the St. Marys River.

ABOVE: The *St. Lawrence,* 1976.

RIGHT, TOP LEFT: The *William A. Irvin* above the Soo Locks in 1977.

RIGHT, TOP RIGHT: The *Henry Phipps,* one of the early 600 footers, above the Locks in 1974.

RIGHT, BOTTOM: The *Eugene W. Pargny* in the fog.

ABOVE: The *Algosound* upbound above the Soo.

RIGHT, TOP: The *Algoma Montrealais* in the St. Clair River, September 2012.

RIGHT, BOTTOM: The *Algocen*, November 1989.

ABOVE: The *A.S. Glossbrenner* off Port Weller Pier, the Welland Canal.

LEFT: The *Edward L. Ryerson* on a December day.

ABOVE: The steamer *William A. Reiss*.

RIGHT, TOP: The *Fort Henry*.

RIGHT, BOTTOM: Spring ice does not slow down the *Royalton*.

FAR RIGHT: The *Ashland* departing the Locks on a winter's day.

ABOVE, LEFT: The *Charles M. Schwab,* which became the *Pierson Daughters* and later the *Beechglen.*

ABOVE, RIGHT: The *Beechglen,* formerly *Pierson Daughters.*

RIGHT, TOP LEFT: The *Pierson Daughters* with a small pilot house.

RIGHT, TOP RIGHT: The *Pierson Daughters* at the Soo with a larger pilot house.

RIGHT, BOTTOM: The *Pierson Daughters* in 1977 from the Blue Water Bridge.

ABOVE: The *Quedoc* at the Soo, May 1976.

LEFT, TOP: The steamer *John P. Reiss.*

LEFT, BOTTOM: The small steamer *Joe S. Morrow* downbound at Mission Point below the Soo Locks.

TOP: The *Judith M. Pierson* downbound at Port Huron on a fall day in 1981.

BOTTOM LEFT: The *Judith M. Pierson* at the Welland Canal.

BOTTOM RIGHT: The *Judith M. Pierson*, formerly the *Silver Bay*, on her last voyage with that name, 1982.

ABOVE: The *Howard F. Andrews* at the Welland Canal.   **FOLLOWING PAGE:** The *Robert S. Pierson* from Port Weller Pier.

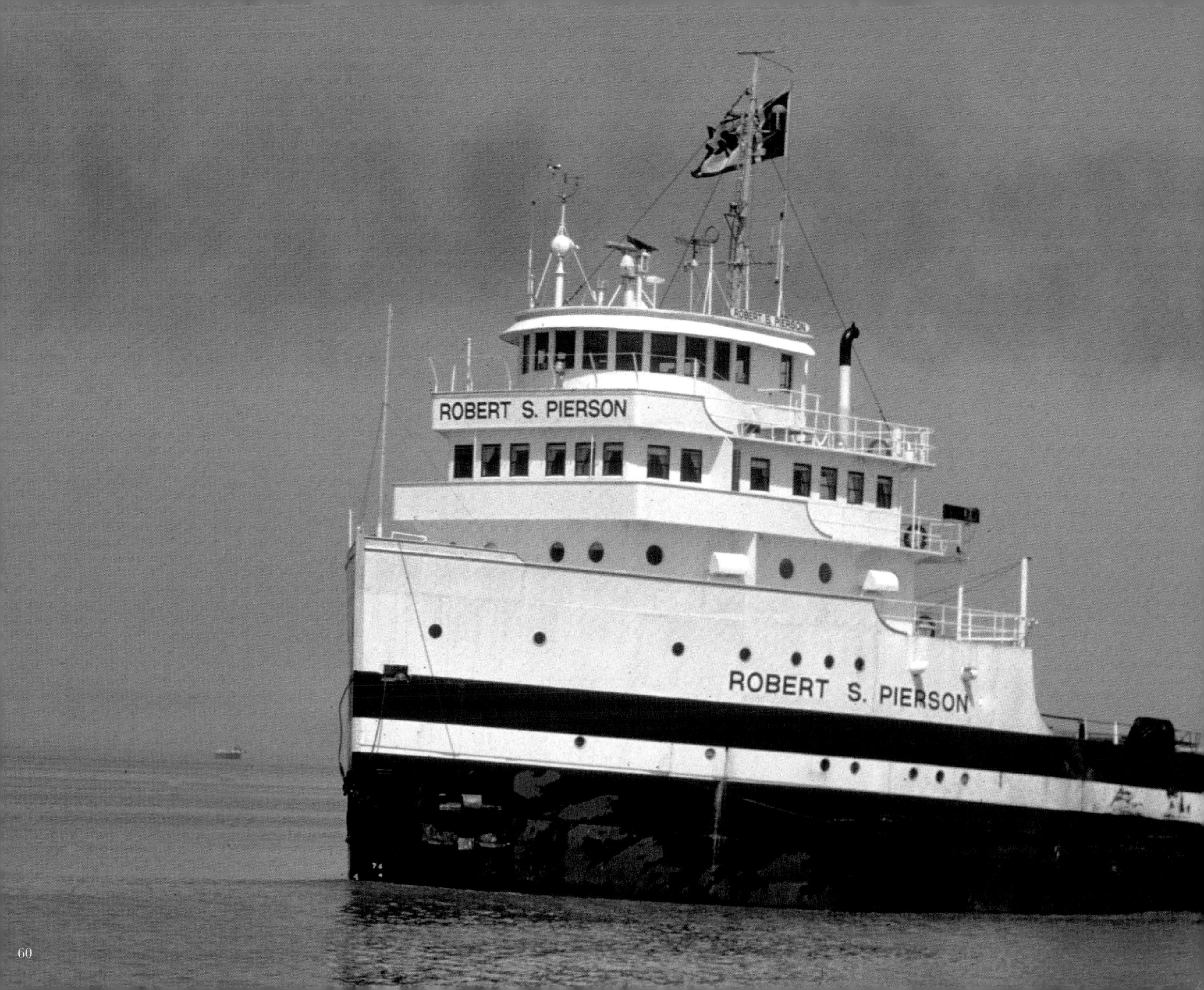

SOO RIVER COMPANY

ABOVE: The *Ben Moreell*.

RIGHT, TOP LEFT: The *Scott Misener* at the Welland Canal 1988.

RIGHT, TOP RIGHT: The *Ralph Misener*.

RIGHT, BOTTOM: The *Scott Misener* at the Blue Water Bridge, Port Huron, Michigan.

ABOVE: The *Champlain* of Cleveland Cliffs.
RIGHT: The *Cliffs Victory* at the Soo, 1976.

ABOVE: The *Benson Ford* and Sugar Island ferry.

RIGHT, TOP LEFT: The *Benson Ford* at dusk.

RIGHT, TOP RIGHT: The *Benson Ford* at Mission Point below the Soo Locks.

RIGHT, BOTTOM: The *Benson Ford* downbound on the St. Marys River, May 1977.

ABOVE: The *Ernest R. Breech* of Ford Motor Company loading grain at Superior, Wisconsin.

LEFT, TOP: The *William Clay Ford* at the Soo in 1975.

LEFT, BOTTOM: The *Canadian Hunter.*

TOP LEFT: The *Paul H. Carnahan* downbound at the Sugar Island Ferry.

TOP RIGHT: The *Charles M. Beeghly.*

BOTTOM LEFT: The *Rimouski.*

BOTTOM RIGHT: The *Harry Coulby,* 1980.

RIGHT: The *Baie St. Paul* going out into stormy Lake Ontario.

ABOVE: The *Meaford* at the Sarnia, Ontario, grain elevator.

LEFT: The *Thornhill* at the start of the 1974 season.

ABOVE: The *Seaway Queen* and the *Goderich*.

RIGHT, TOP LEFT: The *Seaway Queen* with ice.

RIGHT, TOP RIGHT: The *Seaway Queen* stern view.

RIGHT, BOTTOM: The *H. C. Heimbecker* of 1905 upbound in 1981.

ABOVE: The *Canadian Miner* loading grain at Superior, Wisconsin.

RIGHT: The *Canadian Provider* at the Welland Canal.

ABOVE: The *Cartiercliffe Hall* at the Welland Canal.

LEFT, TOP LEFT: The *Merle M. McCurdy*, 1980.

LEFT, TOP RIGHT: The *Lehigh*.

LEFT, BOTTOM: The *William A. McGonagle* unloads cargo at Superior, Wisconsin in 1985.

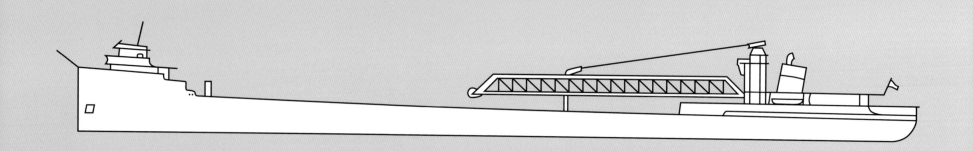

BULK CARRIERS CONVERTED INTO SELF-UNLOADERS

Conversion of Great Lakes ships from bulk freighters to self-unloaders was a common occurrence dating back to the first self-unloader, the *Hennipen*. In the 1920s, with the increasing demand for coal to heat homes and stone for construction, many bulk carriers were converted to self-unloaders. The 1950s and early '60s saw more conversions to accommodate stone cargoes. The 1897-built *Niagara* was a straight decker until conversion to a self-unloading sand boat in 1957.

In the late 1960s, the once plentiful deposits of raw iron ore became depleted. The fringe area of the quarries contained a lower grade of ore which at one time was thought to be unusable. However a process was developed which would merge the lower grade ore and limestone to form taconite pellets. The self-unloading ships, particularly the thousand footers, could unload these pellets to the steel mills more easily and with a faster unloading time. Soon the older system of hulett unloaders with clamps became obsolete. As a result many bulk carriers were converted to self-unloaders in the 1970s and early '80s. This section will include photographs of ships converted from bulkers to self-unloaders during these years.

The *Henry Ford II* was one of the first converted in 1974 with the self-unloader mounted behind the forward cabins. Many were to follow, such as *Wilfred Sykes* and *Herbert C. Jackson* in 1975, with the self-unloader placed aft, ahead of the stern cabins. Others included vessels of Cleveland Cliffs iron company, Columbia Transportation, and United States Steel's Great Lakes Fleet. Some of the converted vessels from these years are no longer in service today. Others such as Great Lakes Fleet's *Clarke*, *Anderson*, and *Callaway* haul stone to ports around the lakes while the thousand footers supply taconite to the steel mills.

ABOVE: The *Armco* as a bulker, 1975, before lengthening.

RIGHT: The *Armco* converted to a self-unloader.

ABOVE: The steamer *Middletown* as a bulk carrier.

BELOW: The *Herbert C. Jackson* as a bulker.

ABOVE: The steamer *Middletown* as a self-unloader.

ABOVE: The *Philip R. Clarke* as a bulk carrier, 1977, at the Soo.

ABOVE: The *Philip R. Clarke* as a self-unloader.

BELOW: The *Herbert C. Jackson* as a self-unloader.

ABOVE: The *Cason J. Callaway* as a self-unloader, Port Huron, September 2013.

LEFT: The *Cason J. Callaway as a bulker*, downbound on the St. Marys River sporting her 1976 bicentennial colors.

ABOVE, LEFT: The *Sparrows Point* as a bulker.

ABOVE, RIGHT: The *Sparrows Point* as a self-unloader.

BELOW: The *Reserve* as a self-unloader on the St. Marys River, 1988.

LEFT: The *Reserve* as a bulker on St. Marys River, 1979.

ABOVE: The *Benson Ford*, formerly the *Edward B. Greene*.

LEFT, TOP: The *Edward B. Greene* of Cleveland Cliffs as a bulker.

LEFT, BOTTOM: The *Edward B. Greene* as a self-unloader.

TOP: The *Walter A. Sterling,* as a bulker, at Mission Point, Sault Ste. Marie, 1974.

BOTTOM: The *Walter A. Sterling,* as a self-unloader, at Point Edward, Ontario, 1980.

TOP: The *Henry Ford II*, as a bulker, 1972 at the Soo.

BOTTOM: The *Henry Ford II*, as a self-unloader.

ABOVE: The *Quetico*, formerly the *Whitefish Bay*, as a self-unloader at the Soo.

LEFT, TOP: The *Whitefish Bay* in April 1968, in her original configuration as a bulk carrier.

LEFT, BOTTOM: The *Quetico* was reconverted back to a bulker and renamed the *Whitefish Bay*. This is her first voyage after reconversion, April 1983.

ABOVE: The *Wilfred Sykes* tied up awaiting upbound passage through the Soo Locks ,1974.

RIGHT, TOP LEFT: The *Wilfred Sykes* as a bulker in the MacArthur Lock at the Soo, 1974.

RIGHT, TOP RIGHT: The *Wilfred Sykes* as a self-unloader at Muskegon.

RIGHT, BOTTOM LEFT: The *Wilfred Sykes* in bicentennial colors.

RIGHT, BOTTOM RIGHT: The *Wilfred Sykes* as a self-unloader in ice, 1980.

ABOVE: The *Courtney Burton*, formerly the *Ernest T. Weir*, as a self-unloader.

LEFT: The *Ernest T. Weir*, as a bulker, downbound at the Blue Water Bridge at Port Huron, Michigan, 1978.

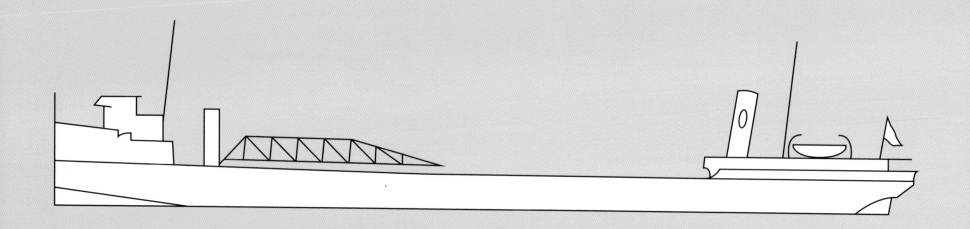

SELF-UNLOADERS

The origin of the self-unloader is attributed to the development of the limestone industry around 1900. Limestone is used in conjunction with the steel industry. Other uses include road building, construction, as well as being an important ingredient in the making of glass. The *Hennepin*, a wooden steamer built in 1888 is known to be the first self-unloader, being converted in 1901. The self-unloader system combines conveyor belts, buckets, and a swinging boom to transfer cargo from ship to a dock. This design by the Webster manufacturing company of Chicago was crude but led the way for more sophisticated unloading systems in the future.

Early self-unloaders were built for the Michigan Alkali Company beginning in 1908 with the steel steamer *Wyandotte*. The Pittsburgh Glass Plate Company with plants along the lower Detroit River hired Michigan Alkali to haul limestone down from the limestone rich area along the Michigan shores of northern Lake Huron.

In the first years of the twentieth century, the steel mills along the lower lakes were feeling the need for more limestone as local quarries were being depleted. A large area of limestone was discovered in 1907 near the small Lake Huron town of Rogers City. The Michigan Limestone Company was founded for the sole purpose of bringing stone to the mills of United States Steel at Gary, Indiana. Their first self-unloaders were the *Calcite* of 1912 and the *W.F. White* of 1915. Over the years they had many self-unloaders built including the *Carl D. Bradley* of 1927, a giant at 639 feet. The *Bradley*, however, met an untimely end in a Lake Michigan gale in November 1958.

The popularity of self-unloaders has increased over the years. Many other shippers turned to the self-unloader to haul stone, coal, or potash. Specialty self-unloaders such as the *Niagara* of 1897, *Sand Merchant*, and *Charles Dick* were used to carry sand, which is sometimes used in the auto business. Eventually self-unloaders dominated the iron ore trade as pelletized ore is more easily discharged by the self-unloader.

273T. CALCITE. PESHA PHOTO.

ABOVE: The *Calcite*, built 1912.   PHOTO: ACHESON VENTURES, VANDERLINDEN COLLECTION.

LEFT: The *Hennepin*, the first self-unloader.   PHOTO: ACHESON VENTURES, VANDERLINDEN COLLECTION.

ABOVE: The *W. F. White*, early Bradley self-unloader.

RIGHT: The *McKee Sons* in the St. Marys River, May 1975.

BELOW, LEFT: The *T. W. Robinson*.

BELOW, RIGHT: The *Mississagi*.

ABOVE: The *Saginaw*, formerly the *John J. Boland*.

LEFT, TOP: The *John J. Boland* at the Soo, 1974.

LEFT, MIDDLE: The *Saginaw* at Port Huron.

LEFT, BOTTOM: The *Saginaw* down bound on the St. Clair River.

FAR LEFT: The *Jean Parisien* at the Welland Canal.

ABOVE: The *Silverdale* at the Welland Canal.

LEFT, TOP: The *Leadale* unloading stone at Welland Canal, 1974.

LEFT, BOTTOM: The *Avondale* at the Welland Canal.

FAR LEFT: The *Leadale* at Welland Canal, 1975.

ABOVE: The *Niagara* sand boat in the Saginaw River at Bay City.

RIGHT, TOP: The *Canadian Pioneer*.

RIGHT, BOTTOM: The *Arthur M. Anderson* on the St. Clair River.

ABOVE: The *Hon. Paul Martin* from the Blue Water Bridge.

LEFT, TOP LEFT: The *Myron C. Taylor* docking at the Soo to unload stone.

LEFT, TOP RIGHT: The *Myron C. Taylor* downbound on the St. Marys River.

LEFT, BOTTOM: The *Myron C. Taylor.*

ABOVE: The *G.A. Tomlinson* unloading stone at Sarnia, Ontario, October 1975.

RIGHT: The *Conallison* at the Welland Canal.

ABOVE: The *Canadian Transport* on Lake St. Clair as seen from the steamer *Beechglen*, 1988.

LEFT, TOP: The steamer *Buckeye* on the St. Marys River, 1978.

LEFT, BOTTOM: The steamer *Buckeye* in the ice.

ABOVE: The *William R. Roesch*.

RIGHT, TOP LEFT: The *Adam E. Cornelius*.

RIGHT, TOP RIGHT: The *Diamond Alkali* at the Soo, November 1974.

RIGHT, BOTTOM: The *John G. Munson* on a winter's day.

ABOVE: The *Joseph H. Frantz* unloading coal at Superior, Wisconsin.

RIGHT: The steamer *Nicolet* leaving Grand Haven.

CEMENT CARRIERS

As the Great Lakes region grew, the demand for cement to build towns, cities, and roads found a ready supply of limestone along its shores. In 1907, Huron Portland Cement was formed in a partnership between J.B. Ford and S.T. Crapo to mine and produce cement at Alpena, Michigan, on Lake Huron. The early ships to haul cement were package freighters such as the *Scranton*. The cement was shipped in bags and could not keep up with the demand.

In 1916, an older Great Lakes bulk carrier, the *Samuel Mitchell*, was purchased and converted to carry cement in bulk. This ship was so successful Huron had two vessels built exclusively for this cargo, the *John W. Boardman* (later *Lewis G. Harriman*) in 1923 and the *S.T. Crapo* in 1927. Huron's fleet continued to grow with the demand, and older freighters were converted to cement carriers whether they had served on the lakes or in ocean service. They were named *J.B. Ford*, *E.M. Ford*, *J.A.W. Iglehart*, and the *Paul H. Townsend*.

The Petoskey Cement Co. (later Penn-Dixie), located at its namesake port, and the Medusa Cement Co., just to the south at Charlevoix, also involved older Great Lakes ships in the production of cement. Huron Cement (now Lafarge North America), however, used the inland seas the most in shipping cement.

Some of the cement carriers on the Great Lakes are of note because of their longevity. These vessels operated for a single purpose, so there was much less wear and tear compared to conventional lakers. The first cement carrier, the *Samuel Mitchell*, was almost 100 years old when it was scrapped. Another converted laker, the 1898-built *E.M. Ford*, was towed for eventual dismantling in 2011. The *J.B. Ford*, built in 1904, sits in retirement awaiting her fate. In 2014, the 1906-built *St. Mary's Challenger* ended her days as a steamer to become a barge for further service. Some cement carriers spent their last years in cement storage, like the 1927-built *S.T. Crapo*, increasing their longevity. The oldest currently operating cement carrier is the *Alpena*, which started out as the ore carrier *Leon Fraser*, built in 1942, then converted for this use in 1990. Others could be cited, but this special-purpose vessel has an interesting history, not just on the American side of the Great Lakes but the Canadian side as well. The cement carrier is a vessel with a history and a future.

ABOVE: The *Samuel Mitchell*, first cement carrier in 1916.
PHOTO: ACHESON VENTURES, VANDERLINDEN COLLECTION.

RIGHT, TOP LEFT: The *J.A.W. Iglehart* on the St. Marys River, 1983.

RIGHT, TOP RIGHT: The *J.B. Ford* blowing the steam whistle.

RIGHT, BOTTOM: The *Lewis G. Harriman* from the Blue Water Bridge, 1978.

ABOVE: The *Southdown Challenger*.

BELOW: The *Southdown Challenger* upbound at Port Huron.

LEFT, TOP: The *E.M. Ford* at Port Huron, Michigan, 1975.

LEFT, BOTTOM LEFT: The *E.M. Ford* laid up at Bay City, Michigan.

LEFT, BOTTOM RIGHT: The *E.M. Ford* engine room.

ABOVE: The *S.T. Crapo* departing the cement dock at Muskegon.

RIGHT, TOP: The *S.T. Crapo* entering Muskegon, Michigan, channel.

RIGHT, BOTTOM: The *S.T. Crapo* on the St. Clair River, March 1991.

LEFT: The *S.T. Crapo* leaving St. Joseph, Michigan.

ABOVE: The *Paul H. Townsend* leaving Muskegon, Michigan.

RIGHT: The *Paul H. Townsend* at Muskegon, Michigan.

LEFT, TOP LEFT: The *Leon Fraser*.

LEFT, TOP RIGHT: Aboard *Alpena*, formerly the *Leon Fraser*, at its open house showing the unloading system.

LEFT, BOTTOM: The newly converted cement boat *Alpena* on her first trip from the shipyard at Superior, Wisconsin, 1991.

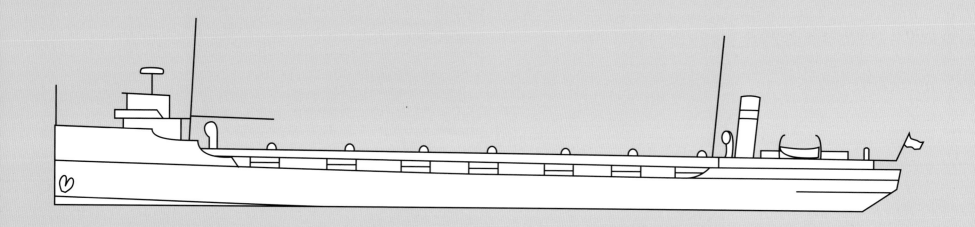

OIL TANKERS

The transportation of oil on the Great Lakes began with the formation of Standard Oil of Ohio by John D. Rockefeller in 1870. Standard would become the largest shipper of oil and kerosene in the country. Kerosene was developed in the 1850s as an alternative to whale oil for lamps and home heating. Rockefeller was aware of the relative ease and cost effective means of transporting his product by water. At first, kerosene was shipped in barrels and later by barge. In 1896, refineries were set up in Cleveland and along the southern shore of Lake Michigan at Whiting, Indiana, for the refinement of oil. A large tank farm was built at Superior, Wisconsin, from which pipelines could carry oil throughout the upper Midwest. That year the first shipment of oil from Whiting to Superior arrived by barge. Standard's first steam tanker, the *Renown*, was built in 1912. Five more beautiful steam tankers would be built in the ensuing years concluding with the *Red Crown* of 1937. The oil shipments from Whiting would continue until the 1980s.

Other American oil shippers were Texaco and Cleveland Tankers. The Cleveland Tanker steamer *Meteor*, a former bulker, became the only whaleback to be converted to carry oil. She now resides as a museum ship in Superior, Wisconsin.

On the Canadian side, the Imperial Oil Company Ltd. began hauling oil products in the late 1890s. The *Imperial* of 1898 was the first self-propelled tanker on the Great Lakes. Other Canadian companies included the British American company as well as Texaco Canada and Shell.

By the 1980s, all the handsome steam tankers had been retired. The increased use of pipelines as well as more stringent safety standards for the transport of oil led to a downturn of shipping oil on the lakes. Bulk transport of oil is now done mainly by tug barge on the American side. Canada still transports oil in diesel tankers. The Canadians have had an especially rich heritage of shipping by tankers on the Great Lakes and continue to do so today.

134

ABOVE: The *L. Rochette.*

RIGHT, TOP LEFT: The *Gulf Canada.*

RIGHT, TOP RIGHT: The *Coastal Canada,* formerly the *Gulf Canada.*

RIGHT, BOTTOM: The *Cape Transport,* 1968.

ABOVE: The *Imperial Sarnia*.

LEFT, TOP: The *Imperial Collingwood* at Port Huron, 1975.

LEFT, BOTTOM: The *Seaway Trader*, formerly *Imperial Collingwood*, at Welland Canal.

ABOVE: The wood wheel on the *Texaco Brave*.

LEFT: The *Texaco Chief*.

143

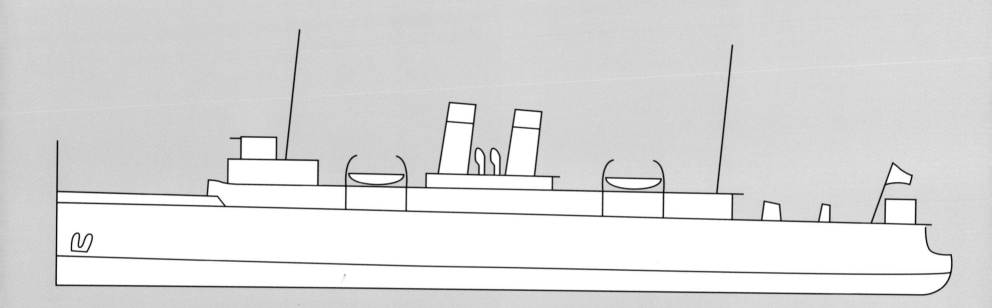

CAR FERRIES

One of the earliest Great Lakes car ferries was the *St. Ignace*, which crossed the Straits of Mackinac between Mackinaw City and St. Ignace. The developing railroad system in the 1870s stretched across Michigan's Upper Peninsula to reach St. Ignace. The rail lines also ran north from the more populated Lower Peninsula to reach Mackinaw City.

The development of the lumber and mining industry made it necessary for the shipments of goods across the Straits, with principle cargoes of lumber and copper. In 1887 the Mackinac Transportation Company ordered the building of the ferry *St. Ignace* with a bow propeller to break ice. A larger ferry, the *Sainte Marie I* was built in 1893. In 1911 the most famous of the ice breaking ferries was built, the *Chief Wawatam*, followed by a slightly smaller ferry, the *Sainte Marie II*, in 1913. The *Chief Wawatam* was a highly successful ferry and ice breaker for years.

On Lake Michigan, three major car ferry companies operated from Michigan ports: The Ann Arbor out of Frankfort, Pere Marquette of Ludington, and the Grand Trunk at Grand Haven, later Muskegon. Frankfort and Ludington were important areas for lumbering, which attracted the railroads. In 1892, the Toledo, Ann Arbor & Northern Michigan Railroad reached Frankfort. The railroad began to operate what were called "Break Bulk" cargoes across Lake Michigan, which were off-loaded from trains onto the boats. This was a time-consuming process, and James Ashley envisioned ferries to carry loaded railcars across the lake. Two wooden ferries were designed by Frank Kirby and built in 1892. There were the *Ann Arbor No. 1 and No. 2*. Thereafter, the Pere Marquette and Grand Trunk followed with ferries crossing Lake Michigan. The Pere Marquette eyed the developments in Frankfort and had a large steel ferry built named *Pere Marquette* in 1896. The first Grand Trunk ferry was the *Grand Haven* of 1903.

Over the years the Pere Marquette would have the most cross-lake ferries. As of 1927 the Pere Marquette had eight, the Ann Arbor five, and Grand Trunk four. In the 1930s, the Pere Marquette added much larger and powerful ferries such as the *City of Saginaw 31, City of Flint 32* and *City of Midland 41*. Even after this fleet became part of the Chesapeake & Ohio in 1947, the building of larger ferries continued with the *Spartan* of 1952 and the *Badger* of 1953. After 1970, the use of ferries declined with better rail service around Lake Michigan through Chicago. Although Chesapeake & Ohio continues to serve, the Ann Arbor and Grand Trunk ceased operations. Finally, the C&O stopped and sold their ferries into private hands.

The *Badger* was converted to an automobile carrier and continues to serve in this trade between Ludington, Michigan, and Manitowoc, Wisconsin, a reminder of a bygone era. Of the large railroad ferries on the Great Lakes, one would survive 75 years as a steamer, the *Chief Wawatam* of 1911. After 1978 she saw limited service. When the St. Ignace dock collapsed in 1986, the end came. Her engines would no longer smoke at the straits.

ABOVE: The *Chief Wawatam* approaching Mackinaw City.

LEFT, TOP: The *Chief Wawatam* at the Mackinaw City dock, 1979.

LEFT, BOTTOM: The Soo Line caboose with the *Chief Wawatam*.

RIGHT: The *Chief Wawatam* with white steam and black smoke.

ABOVE, TOP: The *Chief Wawatam* coming to the Mackinaw City dock.

ABOVE, BOTTOM: The *Chief Wawatam* heading for Mackinaw City.

LEFT: The *Chief Wawatam* at St. Ignace being unloaded by Soo Line engines.

ABOVE, TOP: The *Chief Wawatam* on a cold morning.

ABOVE, BOTTOM: The *Chief Wawatam* at St. Ignace, 1977.

RIGHT: The *Chief Wawatam* displays her signature plume as she battles the ice.

ABOVE: The Grand Trunk car ferry *Madison* laid up at Muskegon, Michigan, 1974.

LEFT: The *City of Midland 41* leaving Ludington, Michigan, 1983.

ABOVE: The *Spartan*.

RIGHT, TOP: The *Viking* coming to Frankfort, 1980.

RIGHT, BOTTOM: The *Viking*, as seen from the *City of Milwaukee*.

ABOVE: The *Badger* departing at sunset.

RIGHT, TOP: The *Badger* at Ludington, 2004.

RIGHT, MIDDLE: The *Badger* approaching Manitowoc.

RIGHT, BOTTOM: The *Badger* at dusk.

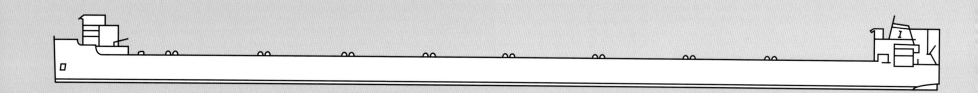

SUPER SHIPS

Ever since the rush to get iron ore to the steel mills during World War II, lake shippers have envisioned super carriers. The maximum size of a Great Lakes freighter is contingent upon the size of the locks at the Soo. Of the five locks at the Soo in 1945, the MacArthur was the newest with dimensions of 800 feet long and 80 feet wide. The other four had longer lengths but shallow drafts and were deemed inadequate. By the end of the war it was generally thought that vessel lengths had stabilized at 640 feet. However, in 1949 the *Wilfred Sykes* came out at 678 feet long and would later be followed by vessels reaching 730 feet long.

In 1946, plans for a larger lock were approved, but funding was not available until 1958. Construction began on the new Poe lock in 1960 that, when completed, would allow passage for ships 1000 feet long. The era of the Super Ships was about to begin with plans to build ships 1000 feet long and 105 feet wide. U.S. Steel ordered a vessel 858 feet long by 105 feet wide, the *Roger Blough*, feeling that a thousand footer would not be able to navigate the St. Marys River well. Bethlehem steel thought otherwise and built the first thousand footer on the lakes, the *Stewart J. Cort*, sailing its maiden voyage in May 1972. The second thousand footer was the tug barge *Presque Isle* coming

out in 1973, with U.S. Steel managing it. Within ten years, ten more thousand footers were built with cabins in the stern, unlike the *Cort* and *Blough* with cabins at the bow and stern in the traditional Great Lakes design.

Of the Super Ships built between 1972 and 1981, the *William J. Delancy*, now the *Paul R. Tregurtha*, is the biggest at 1013 feet long, 105 feet wide, with a depth of 56 feet. This and the other Super Ships exclusively haul cargos of ore and coal to specific ports and places. The capacity of these ships is about 58,000 tons per trip, which is three to four times that of an older 600-foot ship. These thousand-foot ships, including the *Roger Blough*, are a unique breed of ship and are awesome to behold on our inland seas!

ABOVE: The *Indiana Harbor* leaves the Muskegon, Michigan, channel heading for Lake Michigan.

LEFT: The *Mesabi Miner* downbound at Port Huron passing under the Blue Water Bridge.

ABOVE: The *Oglebay Norton* loading coal at Superior, Wisconsin.

RIGHT, TOP: The *Edgar B. Speer* in the rock cut below the Soo, 2012.

RIGHT, BOTTOM: The *Edgar B. Speer* as seen from the *Kinsman Enterprise*.

ABOVE: The *Roger Blough*. shown rounding Whitefish Point in October 2016.

LEFT: The *Roger Blough* shown at the Soo in October 1972, her first year in service.

ABOVE: The *Stewart J. Cort* passing Mackinac Island.

RIGHT, TOP LEFT: The *Stewart J. Cort* loading taconite at Burlington Northern Elevator, September 1993.

RIGHT, TOP RIGHT: The *Stewart J. Cort* upbound at the Soo, December 1994.

RIGHT, BOTTOM: The *Stewart J. Cort* entering the rock cut below the Soo, October 1994.

167

ABOVE: Thousand footer *James R. Barker* off Duluth piers.

LEFT, TOP LEFT: The *James R. Barker* upbound on Lake Huron.

LEFT, TOP RIGHT: The *James R. Barker* in the St. Marys River.

LEFT, BOTTOM: The *Columbia Star* in the rock cut below the Soo.

ABOVE: The *George A. Stinson.*

RIGHT: The *Belle River* leaving Duluth.

CANADA

Lake Superior

MINNESOTA

MICHIGAN

Lake Michigan

Lake Huron

WISCONSIN

St. Lawrence River

MAINE

VERMONT

NEW HAMPSHIRE

MASSACHUSETTS

Lake Ontario

NEW YORK

RHODE ISLAND

Lake Erie

IOWA

CONNECTICUT

PENNSYLVANIA

ILLINOIS   INDIANA   OHIO

NEW JERSEY

DELAWARE

DC

WEST
VIRGINIA

MARYLAND

MISSOURI

VIRGINIA

KENTUCKY

ST. LAWRENCE SEAWAY

The opening of the St. Lawrence Seaway had a profound effect upon Great Lakes shipping. In 1895 the Canadian and American governments appointed the first of many studies for developing a deep water passage from the Atlantic Ocean to the Great Lakes. In all, a series of four Welland Canal systems around the Niagara Falls were built with the newest finished in 1932. There was still a need for a lock system to bypass the various rapids of the St. Lawrence River.

A seaway treaty was signed in 1932 between the U.S. and Canada which had high local interest but failed ratification in the U.S. Senate. Talk of a seaway again surfaced in 1940, but World War II intervened. Finally, the Canadian Parliament voted to start construction in 1951 and the United States joined in by 1954. The locks would replace an antiquated system of smaller locks about 260 feet in length and allow for vessels of 730 feet to travel from Montreal all the way to the head of Lake Superior.

Large ocean vessels could sail from various Great Lake ports such as Chicago, Milwaukee, and Duluth with cargoes destined for overseas. One of the principle cargoes was grain from the Canadian and U.S. heartland. For Canada, the seaway meant smooth transport of grain in 730-foot carriers from the western lakes all the way to Montreal and Quebec City. The Americans had access to the Canadian Labrador ore to supplement the steel industry. Soon new 730 footers would be built for this trade, mostly for Canadian shippers.

The opening of the seaway on April 25, 1959, signaled a new era of Great Lakes shipping. The official opening held at the Eisenhower lock was attended by United States President Dwight D. Eisenhower, Canadian Prime Minister John Diefenbaker, and Queen Elizabeth and Prince Phillip of Great Britain. Celebrations were held in many of the Great Lakes port cities and were highlighted with a tour of the Great Lakes by Queen Elizabeth and Prince Phillip aboard the Royal Yacht *Britannia* and an armada of American naval vessels.

ABOVE: In the Welland canal flight locks.

LEFT: The Royal Yacht *Britannia* at the Soo Locks in 1959 to celebrate the Seaway opening.　*PHOTO RUTH STEVENS.*

ABOVE: The *Grande Hermine*, a Canadian Laker built after the seaway.

LEFT, TOP LEFT: The *Ottercliffe Hall.*

LEFT, TOP RIGHT: The *Quebecois.*

LEFT, BOTTOM: The *Seaway Queen* was launched in 1959 and named to honor the opening of the St. Lawrence Seaway and visit by Queen Elizabeth.

ABOVE: The *Murray Bay* at Port Huron.

RIGHT: The *Roland Desgagnes*, an old canaler.

ROLAND DESGAGNES

ABOVE: The *Texaco Mississippi*.

LEFT, TOP: The *Hutchcliffe Hall*, a canaler originally built to fit the old Seaway.

LEFT, BOTTOM LEFT: The *Federal Saguenay*.

LEFT, BOTTOM RIGHT: The *Mare Sereno* above the Soo Locks.

ABOVE: Salt water ship *Hercegovinia* and the *Kinsman Enterprise* at Superior, Wisconsin, to load grain.

RIGHT: A Welland Canal scene of the *Whitefish Bay* and the *Algocen*.

ABOVE: The *Comeaudoc* at the Welland Canal.

LEFT, TOP: The *City of Newcastle*.

LEFT, BOTTOM: The *Birgit Ragne* from the Mackinac Bridge, 1969.

MUSEUM SHIPS

The fleet of museum ships on the Great Lakes includes four bulk freighters, one whaleback tanker, two passenger ships, a railroad ferry, and one coast guard cutter. The museum ships are the result of foresight on the part of a historical group or, in some cases, an individual to preserve our Great Lakes shipping heritage.

Individuals such as Tom Manse of Sault Ste. Marie, Michigan, led to the saving of the *Valley Camp* from the scrap yard. She has been a museum ship at the Soo since 1968. Another individual, Roland Peterson, bought the retired Canadian passenger steamer *Keewatin* in 1965 and brought her to Saugatuck, Michigan, as a museum. The *Keewatin* is a fine example of a Great Lakes passenger vessel of the early 1900s with beautiful wood furnishings. After many years at Saugatuck, the *Keewatin* was moved to her old home at Port McNicholl, Ontario, in May 2012.

Another passenger vessel which was also an auto carrier is the *Milwaukee Clipper*. She was built as the *Juniata* in 1905 and was modernized and converted to a auto carrier in 1940. Her main route was Muskegon, Michigan, to Milwaukee, Wisconsin, and she was retired in 1970. She now resides as a museum in her old port of Muskegon. The retired railroad ferry *City of Milwaukee* is now a museum in the Lake Michigan town of Manistee, Michigan. The whaleback tanker the *Meteor* is a museum in Superior, Wisconsin.

Besides the *Valley Camp* mentioned above, additional bulk freighters that now serve as museums are the *William A. Irvin*, *William G. Mather*, and *Col. James M. Schoonmaker*. The 1938-built *Irvin* was donated to the city of Duluth, Minnesota, in 1986 by the United States Steel Company. She had sailed forty years in the ore trade before retirement following the 1978 season.

Cleveland Cliffs Company donated two of their retired bulkers to serve as marine museums. They are the steamers *William G. Mather*, which went to Cleveland, and *Willis B. Boyer*, which went to Toledo. The *Boyer* was rechristened in 2010 with her original name *Col. James M. Schoonmaker* and repainted in her original Shenango Company color scheme of green hull and orange boot top. All of the bulk freighter museums have very elaborate living quarters, and we are fortunate that they have been saved from the scrapper's torch.

Lastly, the *Coast Guard Cutter and Ice Breaker Mackinaw* is a museum in Mackinaw City, Michigan. She was built in 1943 and was the most successful icebreaker ever on the Great Lakes. She now sits in view of where she faced her biggest ice breaking battles. These are our museum ships and all are dependent upon many volunteers and support from the general public.

ABOVE: Woodwork aboard the *Keewatin.*

LEFT, TOP: Engine room aboard the *Keewatin.*

LEFT, BOTTOM: Dining room aboard the *Keewatin.*

FAR LEFT: *Keewatin* tow approaching Mackinaw City dock, 2012.

ABOVE, TOP: *William G. Mather* at Cleveland.

ABOVE, BOTTOM: *William G. Mather* officer and guest dining room.

RIGHT: *William G. Mather* at Port Huron, April 1968.

ABOVE: Museum ship *Meteor* at Superior, Wisconsin.

LEFT: Museum ship *William A. Irvin*.

ABOVE: The *City of Milwaukee* in the snow.

RIGHT, TOP LEFT: The *City of Milwaukee*, wheel.

RIGHT, TOP RIGHT: The *City of Milwaukee*, loading the ferry.

RIGHT, BOTTOM LEFT: The *City of Milwaukee*, mid-lake.

RIGHT, BOTTOM RIGHT: The *City of Milwaukee*, engine room builders plate.

STEAMER
CITY OF MILWAUKEE
MANITOWOC SHIP BUILDING CORP.
1931

ABOVE: *Milwaukee Clipper* in original configuration as *Juniata*, 1916.   *PHOTO: ACHESON VENTURES, VANDERLINDEN COLLECTION*

RIGHT: *Milwaukee Clipper* entering Muskegon channel, 1969.

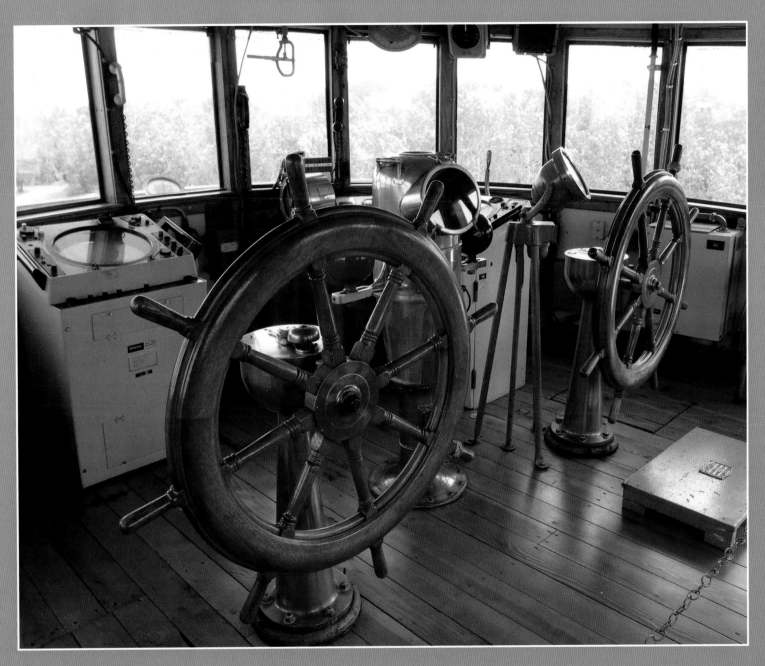

ABOVE: *Col. James M. Schoonmaker* pilot house.

LEFT: *Col. James M. Schoonmaker* at Toledo, Ohio.

ABOVE: The *Silver Bay*, a sister ship to the *Valley Camp*.

RIGHT: The museum ship *Valley Camp*.   PHOTO: *DICK WICKLUND*

MUSEUM SHIP
VALLEY CAMP
Welcome Aboard   ENTRANCE

VALLEY CAMP

ABOVE: *Ice Breaker Mackinaw* as a museum ship at Mackinaw City.

LEFT: *Ice Breaker Mackinaw* at the Soo with a white hull.

203

SHIPBOARD SCENES

The Kinsman fleet was a classic fleet of the Great Lakes which had many interesting and photogenic vessels over the years. The Kinsman fleet was organized in 1901 by Sophia Minch and Henry Steinbrenner. The company was also referred to as the Steinbrenner fleet.

The pictures in this section depict life aboard various Kinsman freighters. They were taken aboard the steamer *Henry Steinbrenner, Kinsman Enterprise*, and *Kinsman Independent*, which were the some of the last vessels to sail for Kinsman. They sailed in the grain business and were among the last straight-deck bulkers to sail for the American fleet. The grain would be loaded in Duluth–Superior at the head of Lake Superior and be brought down to grain elevators at the lower lake ports of Cleveland, Ohio, and Buffalo, New York. The normal sailing time for a round trip would be roughly two weeks.

The *Henry Steinbrenner* was launched in 1916 as the *William A. McGonagle* for the Pittsburgh steamship company, later United States Steel. Kinsman bought the vessel in 1979, and she was renamed *Henry Steinbrenner* in 1986. She was one of the last coal burning freighters to sail the lakes and was retired in 1989.

The *Kinsman Enterprise* was built in 1927 as the *Harry Coulby* for Interlake Steamship and was purchased by Kinsman in 1989. She operated through the 1995 season.

The *Kinsman Independent* was built in 1952 as the *Charles L. Hutchinson* for the Hutchinson Steamship Company. She sailed most of her years with the name *Ernest R. Breech* for Ford Motor Company. Kinsman acquired her in 1988 and sailed her through 2002. She still sails today under the Canadian flag as *Lower Lakes Ojibway*.

I am grateful to Mr. Jake Davis and the Steinbrenner company for allowing me the chance to observe the sailor's way of life as well as photograph these beautiful ships.

LEFT, TOP: Hosing down the deck of grain dust aboard the *Kinsman Enterprise*.

LEFT, BOTTOM: Painting on the *Kinsman Independent*.

ABOVE: Fire and Lifeboat Drill aboard the *Henry Steinbrenner*.

ABOVE: Cooking burgers aboard the *Henry Steinbrenner*.

RIGHT: Mail boat coming out to the *Kinsman Enterprise*.

ABOVE: Pilot house of the *Henry Steinbrenner.*

LEFT, TOP: Plotting the course.

LEFT, BOTTOM: Chess game aboard the *Henry Steinbrenner.*

ABOVE: Wheelman on the *Kinsman Enterprise*.

ABOVE: Flying a kite over Lake Huron.

RIGHT: Scraping out ashes from the boiler on the *Henry Steinbrenner*.

ABOVE: Passing ships on Lake Huron.

LEFT: Stormy seas near Crisp Point on Lake Superior.

ABOVE: The *Kinsman Enterprise* at a Duluth grain elevator.

RIGHT, TOP LEFT: Loading grain into the *Kinsman Independent*.

RIGHT, TOP RIGHT: The *Kinsman Enterprise* leaving Duluth.

RIGHT, BOTTOM LEFT: Foggy morning on the *Kinsman Independent*.

RIGHT, BOTTOM RIGHT: The *Kinsman Enterprise* unloading at Buffalo.

217

ABOVE: Rainstorm on Lake Superior.

LEFT: The shadow of the *Henry Steinbrenner* cast on a fog bank by the rising sun on the St. Marys River, 1988.

ABOVE: Leaving Duluth aboard the *Henry Steinbrenner*.

RIGHT, TOP: The *Roger Blough* in the Poe Lock as seen from the *Henry Steinbrenner*

RIGHT, BOTTOM: The *Roger Blough* raised with *Henry Steinbrenner* low in the Lock.

ABOVE AND LEFT: Owl resting on the *Kinsman Enterprise* nine miles off Alpena.

RIGHT: Sunrise downbound on Lake Superior.

SUNSET FROM BIRCH POINT AT THE LOWER END OF WHITEFISH BAY.

POSTLUDE

May this book be an enjoyment to the casual observer of ships on our Great Lakes.

To former sailors may it bring back memories of gentle breezes and breathtaking sunsets.

The watchman peers from the bow of the *Kinsman Enterprise*
over a foggy St. Clair River in September 1989.

INDEX

BIBLIOGRAPHY & SUGGESTED READING

Ahoy and Farewell, The Marine Historical Society of Detroit, 2001.

Barry, James P., *Ships of the Great Lakes*, Thunder Bay Press, 1973.

Beck, Bill and Patrick Labadie, *Pride of the Inland Seas*, 2004.

Bowen, Dana T., *Lore of the Lakes*, Freshwater Press,1940.

Bowen, Dana T., *Memories of the Lakes*, Freshwater Press, 1946.

Bowen, Dana T., *Shipwrecks of the Great Lakes*, Freshwater Press.

Brown Jr., Grant, *Ninety Years Crossing Lake Michigan*.

Demos, Steven S. and Marylouise Plant, *The S.S. Milwaukee Clipper*.

Dewar, Gary, *Canadian Bulk Construction 1960–1970*, Inland Seas, Quarterly Journal of the Great Lakes Historical Society, Vol. 43 Summer 1987–no. 2.

Kruse, Richard J., *The Silver Stackers*, Freshwater Press.

Lafferty, William and Valarie Van Heest, *Buckets and Belts Evolution of the Great Lakes Self-Unloader*, 2009.

Lapinski, Patrick, *Behemoths of the Lakes, The Age of the 1000-footers*, Lake Superior Magazine, November 2008.

Lapinski, Patrick, *The Whiting Express*, Duluth Seaway Port Authority, North Star Port winter 2009-10.

Metz, Captain Richard D., *Life Aboard A Laker From 1964 to 1999*.

Micketti, Gerald F. and Mark Thompson, *Calcite and the Bradley Boats*, 2012.

Wicklund, Dick and Skip Gillham, *The Kinsman Lines*

ABOUT THE AUTHOR

Bob Campbell became interested in the ships of the Great Lakes at a very young age. In the early 1950s, vacation trips to visit relatives at Sault Ste. Marie exposed Bob to the long ships passing through the locks. Bob's Uncle Jerry Campbell worked in the recording room at the locks and would always talk about the boats. The rides across the Straits of Mackinac on the old coal-fired steam-driven ferries before the bridge opened also had a lasting effect upon him. As a teenager, Bob would always pick up the *Know Your Ships* book put out by Tom Manse. Tom helped mold Bob from a boat watcher to a boat photographer.

Bob's photographs have appeared in *Michigan History Magazine* as well as other publications around the Great Lakes region. Bob has also presented multimedia programs with video as well as still pictures depicting the Great Lakes ships to various marine organizations around the lakes.